PROPHETS'
BREAD

SERMONS FOR ADVENT, CHRISTMAS, & EPIPHANY

CYCLE A FIRST LESSON TEXTS

PROPHETS' BREAD

JOHN G. LYNCH

C.S.S. Publishing Co., Inc.
Lima, Ohio

PROPHETS' BREAD
SERMONS FOR ADVENT, CHRISTMAS, AND EPIPHANY

Copyright © 1989 by
The C.S.S. Publishing Company, Inc.
Lima, Ohio

All rights reserved. No part of this publication may be reproduced, stored in a retrieval system, or transmitted in any form or by any means, electronic, mechanical, photocopying, recording, or otherwise, without the prior permission of the publisher. Inquiries should be addressed to: The C.S.S. Publishing Company, Inc., 628 South Main Street, Lima, Ohio 45804.

Library of Congress Cataloging-in-Publication Data

Lynch, John G.
    Prophets' bread: cycle A texts for Advent, Christmas, and Epiphany / John G. Lynch.
      p.   cm.
    ISBN 1-55673-131-0
    1. Bible. O.T.--Meditations.   I. Title.
BS1151.5.L96   1989
242'.33--dc20

89-9943
CIP

9856 / ISBN 1-55673-131-0   PRINTED IN U.S.A.

For
LaLeve Ziemann

Table of Contents

Foreword			9
Introduction			11
Advent 1	*Isaiah 2:1-5*	*Walk in Light*	13
Advent 2	*Isaiah 11:1-10*	*God as Woodcutter*	17
Advent 3	*Isaiah 35:1-10*	*Desert Springs*	21
Advent 4	*Isaiah 7:10-16*	*Ask for a Sign*	25
The Nativity of Our Lord	*Isaiah 9:2-7*	*The Glance of God*	29
Christmas 1	*Isaiah 63:7-9*	*Burning Torches*	33
Christmas 2	*Jeremiah 31:7-14*	*Tears in Ramah*	37
Epiphany	*Isaiah 60:1-6*	*Who Are These Kings?*	41
The Baptism of Our Lord	*Isaiah 42:1-9*	*Given as Light*	45
Epiphany 2	*Isaiah 49:1-7*	*Hid in God*	49
Epiphany 3	*Isaiah 9:1-4*	*Wait and Hope*	53
Epiphany 4	*Micah 6:1-8*	*Micah's Orders*	57
Epiphany 5	*Isaiah 58:3-9a*	*What God Sees*	61
Epiphany 6	*Deuteronomy 30:15-20*	*Daily Choice*	65
Epiphany 7	*Isaiah 49:8-13*	*Never Forgotten*	69
Epiphany 8	*Leviticus 19:1-2, 9-18*	*Boundaries or Frontier*	73
The Transfiguration of Our Lord	*Exodus 24:12-18*	*Six Cloudy Days*	77

Foreword

John Lynch and I have shared a spiritual journey for the last twenty-two years. We met on an isolated hilltop in northern New Jersey. I was a novice in the Congregation of St. Paul; he was returning to America from years of study in Europe. I thought then, "This man, this priest is different!" Since then, over those twenty-two years, he has been my friend, my teacher, my confessor, my pastor, and my prophet. He continues to be all of those and I am grateful — most of the time! I say most of the time because when you spend time with a prophetic person it is disquieting and John Lynch is a prophetic, disquieting provocateur of the Word of God. So was Isaiah. The prophetic person helps us understand, in the deeper waters of doubt and despair, that God is waiting to embrace us with a relentless, infinite, and abiding love. The prophetic person also has the nasty propensity to remind us when we are building our hopes and dreams on sand rather than grounding ourselves in the Word of God.

In his own journeys, John Lynch has seen religious repression in Russia, yet he had a religious experience there. He has seen stifling depression in Europe yet he chose friends who had a vital, fierce love for freedom. He has seen the oppression of comfort in America try to make the Word of God defined and contained like some lifeless museum piece. But he coaxed and cajoled his flock to risk the greater depths of faith, and for a few he was a voice in the wilderness! Such is the charge to God's prophets.

This book contains a message which reaches into the convictions and experience of any midwestern Minnesota farmer whose faith is tied to the land and the seasons with the bitter defeat of drought and the joy of plentiful harvest. It is a message of hope which reaches pimps and whores and street people, such as those in Paris among whom John Lynch ministered while he was in Europe. It is a message of confidence which reaches the lost, confused, identity-conflicted college students and seminarians for whom he was teacher and chaplain in the crisis ridden years of the sixties and early seventies. It is a message that reaches the everyday faithful who thirst for the Word of God.

This is a book about the myriad dimensions of God's sovereignty over us. It is a book which chastens us to ground ourselves in God, understanding further and deeper that revealed self and the hiddenness of divine purpose. It is a book about Isaiah's journey and his vision.

I invite you to risk the expansion of your theological horizons and the boundaries of your faith and read this book.

When you do I hope that you will experience Martin Luther's exhortation to all of us to be "joyful, eager, high spirited and mettlesome in our relationships with God and each other."

>Robert J. Pelrine
>Vice President
>Maryland Institute of
>   Pastoral Counseling, Inc.
>Annapolis, Maryland

Introduction

Late one August night, I walked in a grove of pine trees near the Chesapeake Bay. The night was clear and cool, almost like a December night in Minnesota. Stars twinkled their bright eyes over all the earth, and I felt the joy of God's creation. Suddenly I stopped in my tracks. One star was not twinkling. In fact, it stared at me with an eye red from tears or a long night vigil at a child's crib. That star (probably the planet Mars, I was told later) stopped me because it made me feel like the child in the crib, helpless by myself, but strong with God watching over me. I pray that these meditations on texts from the Old Testament will give you the sense of God's powerful love that I received while writing them. My thanks to all who helped in their preparation, especially Kenne Miller, Diana Mathis, Cherie Loustaunau, Evelyn Grein, and Bob Pelrine.

Isaiah 2:1-5   *Advent 1*

Walk in Light

Far above the cool, clear waters of New York State's Lake George, looms Black Mountain, the highest of the mountains guarding that deep, clear lake. I spent five summers on that lake as a seminarian, traveling many times, as the Iroquois once traveled, under the shadow of that awe-inspiring peak. The winding trail from the lakeshore to its summit has felt the rough leather boots of hikers of a century ago and the soft deerskin moccasins centuries before that. Along the trail runs a brook filled with rainbow trout. Occasionally a black bear will paw along that trail, looking for berries and trout, its snout always in the air for the smell of danger — especially the danger of human presence.

In the forest nothing signals greater danger to the animals than the smell of man. Man brings to the forest not the plowshare but the sword, not the pruning hook but the spear. Man, the hunter. Animals, the hunted. Consequently most animals do not walk the trail by day. Anyone who wants to see the raccoon, the deer, or the bear, should come at dusk as the night begins to fall. Night gives the forest animals the cover they need to survive.

Not so for the human creatures. Humans do better in the light. We need the light to survive.

I once hiked that trail to the top of Black Mountain at four o'clock in the morning. I wanted to watch the sun rise from its summit, so I gave myself plenty of time to get to the top.

Five or six friends went with me on that hike. Stumbling and falling over each other in the darkness, we walked into low-hanging branches and tripped into the stream. We did not do well until the rays of dawn seeped in through the trees to illuminate our path.

Once that light broke through the trees, we came to a large pool. Something moved in the water. We watched and waited until the light grew stronger. A beautiful rainbow trout swam in there, locked in the pool. The stream was shallow that day. There was no place for the trout to go. It tried to hide under a tiny rock ledge, but it was too big to hide. Once the light grew stronger, the trout knew it was trapped. The light was on our side. The darkness had been on the trout's.

We outnumbered the trout six to one. If it swam to one corner of the pool, one of us scared it back to the other. It was easy, once the light came, to scare the fish into our net, and we had a fresh trout for supper that night.

I didn't eat trout that night. I couldn't. I felt terrible that we had not given the fish a fair chance. In the darkness it had been safe, but once the light came, it was all over. The trout was already in the skillet. People survive by day; animals survive by night.

I don't know whether the prophet Isaiah was a hunter or not, but he certainly knew about light. He knew the advantage light gave armies, generals, and kings to defend their cities in ancient Israel. He knew that farmers plowed by day and that vinedressers tended their vines only during the light of day. He knew, too, that people killed each other by day. Humankind used the light for that purpose, too.

When Isaiah stood up, eight centuries before Jesus, to cry forth the Word of the Lord, he stood as God's daytime heartland, "Come, let us walk in the light of the Lord," he said, "The law will go out from Zion, the word of the Lord from Jerusalem." In Isaiah's vision, God's Word went forth from Jerusalem like a blazing torch to give truth to our naturally dark minds. God's Law sparked from Mount Zion to light a pillar of fire to guide us. Without that Law, we would continue only to beat our plowshares into swords and our pruning hooks into spears.

Isaiah knew, as later Jesus proclaimed, that what defiles us comes out of the heart. We all need the light of God's Word and the spark of God's Law if we are to walk in anything but darkness. Left to ourselves, we are not prone to the plowshare or the pruning hook, but to the sword and the spear.

We need instruction from the Lord to walk in his paths. We need God's light.

Earlier in his prophecy, Isaiah threw light on God as a loving father displeased with his children. "Hear, O heavens, and listen, O earth . . . I reared children and brought them up, but they have rebelled against me . . . I will turn my hand against them. I will thoroughly purge away their dross and remove their impurities." (1:2, 25) God did not do that only once, eight centuries before Jesus. It was done in Jesus' time when God's only Son was nailed to the Cross, and again in our lives each day. God treats us like rusty iron and has to burn off our rust. We are tarnished gold to be polished with God's Word and Law.

I once spent some time in a restaurant in Virginia, where many hunters gathered. A young man of eighteen or so walked in ahead of me. He had just shot his first deer. I heard him say to the woman at the cashier's table: "I never killed anything before." Then he sat down with the two older men who had taken him out early that morning to kill his first deer. They talked of hunting a while. Then he left them, went to the telephone and called somebody in town. All he said was, "I killed me a buck, I killed me a buck, I killed me a buck."

His girlfriend came in. He told her the same thing. "I killed me a buck," he said. She wanted to know where it was so she could take a picture. She came back a few minutes later with a color Polariod shot of the dead buck in the back of a pickup truck. The boy went back to the table with the older men, talking of the rigors and rules of good hunting. The boy stayed for a minute, then he left them, stood in the corner, and stared and stared at that picture. He had the most forlorn look on his face. I wondered, what light is going on in that boy's life today? What is he starting to feel today that he never felt before? What is it about killing the buck that has so struck this young man? Was there some rust burned off his iron that day? Some tarnish rubbed off the gold? Or did he grow a little rusty? Was his gold tarnished that day? Left to ourselves we will tarnish each other's gold and rust each other's iron. Only God will restore us. Only God will bring us to walk in the light.

Luther loved the prophet Isaiah. He lectured extensively on this book of the Bible, encouraging those who heard him to learn from the prophet that God is always on our side, but acting in our Lord's own good time. To those of his day who would reduce the Word of God to a simple word game or an intellectual exercise, Luther warned: "For the Gospel does not concern itself with knowledge; it concerns itself with feeling." (LW 16, 30)

Isaiah put it more vividly, but he had the same vision. "Come, let us go up to the mountain of the Lord, to the house of the God of Jacob. He will instruct us in his ways, and we shall walk in His paths . . . come, let us walk in the light of the Lord."

Isaiah 11:1-10   **Advent 2**

God as Woodcutter

I have a long-standing love affair with trees. I love the forests, and I hate to see a tree chopped down. Any tree. I have a ficus tree that has died, but I can't bring myself to cut it down and throw it away.

When I was very young I had a favorite tree. It grew in the middle of a corn field. I looked forward to spring when my mother would pack me and my sisters in our car and drive out to that field to see that tree. It grew there, a stately king in a black loam field, reigning gloriously over the budding corn and soybeans.

When I lived in Washington, D.C. as a seminary professor, I had a room that overlooked a giant elm tree. I could reach out my window to touch its branches. One day I began to notice something strange about that tree. Its leaves drooped. Some of its branches didn't bud forth any more. It lost its leaves early in the fall. Sure enough, the tree was mortally ill with Dutch Elm disease. It had to be cut down. So did all the other elms which graced the front of the building like welcoming royalty as you walked up the path. It was a sad day when the woodcutters came to take down those trees. One of the professors who had been there forty years earlier, when those trees had been planted, wept when the saws hit the timber. I wrote a poem about the loss of those trees.

It's this kind of feeling about trees, a treasuring of their beauty, their majesty, and their stability, that inspired the prophet Isaiah when he cried forth:

> *See, the Lord, the Lord Almighty,*
> *will lop off the boughs with great power.*
> *The lofty trees will be felled,*
> *the tall ones will be brought low.*
> *He will cut down the forest thickets with an ax . . .*
>
> (10:33-34)

Isaiah knew, as later John the Baptizer and Jesus would teach, that sometimes God comes into our lives like a woodcutter, ax in hand, to cut down the trees. For I can grow a forest in my life of my own plantings and think that it is all my doing. I can believe that I am completely in control and that no one will harm me in my forest. In fact, it is not hard to believe that I am rendered invulnerable by the forest constructed of my own good deeds. John the Baptizer shouted out in his day: "Even now the ax is laid to the root of the trees." (Matthew 3:10 RSV) Isaiah, more than seven hundred years before John, cried forth: "The Lord God will cut down the forest thickets with an ax."

What was Isaiah talking about? Why did he stand up to shout such fierce warnings to his people? Why did Jesus and John the Baptizer quote from his prophecies so much? Why have his words inspired such music as parts of Handel's *Messiah*? What kind of a man was he?

Isaiah lived about 750 years before the birth of Jesus, at a time when God's methods for saving his people seemed to be changing. First, God called Abraham to leave his homeland and journey to another land which God would show him. Abraham believed, and thus became the father of many nations. The first step of God's strategy was to fill a man's heart with belief so he could leave his home for a better land. That strategy God worked through Abraham.

Then, when Abraham's descendants fell into bondage in Egypt, God moved to the next stage in his strategy towards his people. He raised for them a strong and powerful leader to do two things: to lead them out of bondage and to give them a law to live by. That man was Moses, who led God's people into freedom and gave them a law — You shall not kill, you shall not steal, remember the sabbath day, to keep it holy.

But the Law was not enough. So God again did something new. He gave his people kings — first Saul, then David, then Solomon. Solomon had been dead for almost two hundred years when Isaiah came along. The kingdom was split asunder. The Assyrian armies were roaring over all that part of the world like lions to the kill.

Plunged into that chaos, Isaiah preached God's newest strategy towards his people. "The root of your identity as God's people," he said, "is not your descendancy from Abraham . . ." John the Baptizer later repeated the same thing when he said, "God can raise up children to Abraham from the very stones of the street." (Matthew 3:9) "Nor is your identity anchored in the Law given you by Moses," Isaiah continued, "there is more. Do not pretend, either, that you need a king like David or Solomon to be God's people. No, your religious identity is not based on blood lines, Laws, or Kings — it is based on the Word of God."

That Word of God, heralded Isaiah, will come into your lives like a woodcutter's ax to cut down the forest of lies you have built up. And God will raise up something new, there is a purpose to it all. As Isaiah said, "A shoot will come up from the stump of Jesse, from his roots a branch will bear fruit." That branch we identify as Jesus.

When God comes in with the ax of his Word, he cuts so that new life may emerge. That is what we need, whether we know it or not. God cuts down the dead wood so a new shoot will come up from the stump, a new branch which will bear fruit.

God then acts in a new, creative way. God's Spirit, that same Spirit which hovered over the chaos at creation and breathed life into the clay, will breathe anew on us . . . "**a Spirit of knowledge and the fear of the Lord.**" God the woodcutter knows why an ax must fell the trees. We are trees in God's garden that he needs to prune from time to time.

In one of his many lectures on the Prophet Isaiah, Luther said:

> *God does not help except in the greatest trouble and in the utmost need. He is, Psalm 9:9 says, 'a stronghold for the oppressed, a stronghold in times of trouble,' so that it may be evident that the matter is managed by the hand of God, not by the plans of men. This is the Christian thing to do, to recognize the acceptable time and day of salvation (cf. 2 Corinthians 6:2), even when it seems to be a day of despair.* From a trunk nearly decayed a little Twig will emerge and grow up and make holy, and it will not be prevented by heat or by rain or by all the powers of the air.
>
> (LW 16, 118)

Luther's "little Twig" was born in Bethlehem two thousand years ago to prune our forests with his death and bring new growth in his Resurrection. Thanks be to God that we have been grafted unto that Branch which is Christ.

Isaiah 35:1-10　　　　　　　　　　　　　　　　Advent 3

Desert Springs

Nothing stings quite like the desert. I remember standing one time in the midst of a desert at high noon, overlooking a large saline lake. It was so hot you could see the shoreline shrinking in front of you, as the sun drew the water into the air. On the far side of this dwindling lake, cattle sought shelter in caves. Only the flamingos feeding on pink larvae in the water stood untouched by the burning heat of the day.

Being in that desert was really a life threatening situation. I could not stay in that sunlight very long. Like the cattle, I too had to seek a cave for shelter or the shade of a divi-divi tree. As I drove through that wilderness, wild parrots and ruby-topaz hummingbirds flew in and out of the cactus, but there was no escaping the relentless heat. There was no real relief to be found anywhere.

At one point in my travels that day I saw a windmill in the distance. It was not one of those gigantic windmills you see in Holland, but one of those spindly things you see over farm wells. As I approached this spindleshanks contraption, I saw that it was in fact a water pump. Some enterprising farmer had actually sunk a well in the desert to draw up fresh water. So miraculous was this water when it hit the surface that a small jungle had grown right in the desert. Banana trees replaced cacti, and even a vegetable garden grew near the well.

All around this little oasis was the burning land, its heat waves shimmering to the sky to warn any living thing that the desert could kill.

The prophet Isaiah, like his counterpart John the Baptizer many years later, knew the desert. He knew the shimmering rays, the mirages, the lakes dwindling in the heat. He knew that some deserts supported plant life only, some were pasture land, and some supported no life. These are the most terrifying of all — and the most lonely.

In fact, in today's section from Isaiah's prophecy, there are three words for desert. We translate them as *wilderness, parched land,* and *desert.* In our hearts, too, we have these three deserts. Human life in itself is wild, parched, and dangerous. God must provide water for our thirst if we are to survive. Left to ourselves, we will smolder in the heat of undifferentiated anger, lost without the waters of God's grace.

Isaiah had first-hand experience of the desert inside. In his time, seven hundred years before Jesus, the Assyrian armies under the leadership of their famous general Sennacherib were destroying all the wells in Judah, devastating the earth, and leaving nothing but desolation, waste, and jackals on the land. In the midst of this devastation, Isaiah stood up to proclaim hope, God's relief to be given like a well sunk in dry land. Other prophets reviled and scorned him as a fool until he himself began to feel like a desert land. He even gathered up his two sons and his wife and took them away for awhile.

When Isaiah came back, he prefaced his hopeful words, some of the most beautiful ever spoken, with this description of how it felt before God sunk his well of hope:

> *God will stretch out over Edom the measuring line of chaos and the plumb line of desolation . . . Thorns will overrun her citadels, nettles and brambles her strongholds. She will become a haunt for jackals, a home for owls.*
> (Isaiah 34:11-13)

Then, as God sunk a well of grace into Isaiah's heart, the prophet cried out:

The desert and the parched land will be glad; the wilderness will rejoice and blossom . . . Water will gush forth in the wilderness and streams in the desert. The burning sand will become a pool, the thirsty ground bubbling springs. In the haunts where jackals once lay, grass and reeds and papyrus will grow.

No one's life is exempt from the measuring line of chaos or the plumb line of desolation. Not one of us is a citadel so strong that thorns or nettles can't grow there. We all feel the jackals and the vultures from time to time. That is precisely when God comes with relief like sinking a well in the desert. God will take over and bring into our thirsty lives the bubbling spring of his consoling and strengthening Word. That is the time to rejoice, as Isaiah rejoiced, when he saw the jackals finally driven from the land.

For us there can be no hopeless situation, no desert without end. There is always the oasis, always the well of God's grace, always the gushing forth of God's loving care.

Luther, too, knew the deserts in life that Isaiah knew. He, too, felt the jackals tearing at his heart, the princes who wanted to burn him at the stake and the philosophers who objected to his raw, deep presentation of the truth. In Luther's day, too, many preferred the wilderness to the sinking of God's wells deep within the heart.

In Luther's commentary on this section of the prophet Isaiah, the intensity of his gift of faith rises like heat waves in the desert.

As a spring flows forth in moistening streams, so this church, which was desert, should gush out in streams of the teachings of the Gospel, always one stream leaping from another into one city and then another, although in the eyes of the world it might seem forever desert . . . The Word of God will come in abundance.

(LW 16, 302-303)

Luther then takes this desert imagery and applies it to his favorite theme: the freedom of the Christian. He builds on the second image that Isaiah uses in today's lesson. After the Lord has refreshed us with the healing and comforting Word, he then builds a highway in the wilderness so that we may travel in his footsteps. "This way will be safe," says Luther, "since the lions, that is, the disturbers and teachers of traditions, will not be there, but sincere pastors of the Gospel . . ." (LW 16, 304)

We will have our desert moments and our wilderness times. We will have the jackals tearing at our hearts from time to time. We will feel there is no road to walk, that each step is dangerous. All this is Word.

Then the Word comes in a fresh way — through a sympathetic listener, whose listening itself is a gushing spring of renewed hope. It comes through a few moments spent reading a prophet like Isaiah, whose poetry and prayer is a highway through a barren land. The Word comes in the comforting, or not so comforting but still truthful, Word that someone whispers to our ears.

God's Word speaks through so many different voices. If sometimes it comes like the jackal's teeth, that is only the prelude to move us to the place where it comes like a rushing stream or a gushing spring. All these voices echo from the Word of God made flesh in Jesus who died and rose to life for us.

Thanks be to God for his freeing and refreshing Word which keeps us on the highway of truth in the midst of our parched and withered lives.

Isaiah 7:10-16　　　　　　　　　　　　　　Advent 4

Ask for a Sign

I asked for my first sign from God in the midst of World War II. We had only been in that war a few months in May of 1942 when that day came for me. In the Far East Admiral Nimitz was directing the first Allied Offensive to stop the Japanese Imperial Navy in the Battle of the Coral Sea, while beginning plans for the more famous Battle of Midway. In North Africa, Field Marshall Von Rommel was still a power, but he would fade as the British planes struck his supply lines and a General named Patton began command of our tank corps there.

That was quite an atmosphere in which to celebrate First Communion. Newspaper headlines told of war. The newsreels at the movies were filled with smoke and explosions, usually of airplanes crashing into the sea. When we played in the leaf piles at the end of the street, we always took on the personalities of World War II generals and admirals. I always wanted to be either General de Gaulle or General Giraud, commander of the Free French in North Africa.

There were wars closer to home, too. Down the street lived two boys who didn't like me very much. For some reason I was their enemy, as were two of my friends. We had to be very careful if we walked to that end of the street. It was more expedient to walk around the block the other way to get to school or to the neighborhood grocery store to buy a Milky Way.

Even at home there was war. By that time, I had two

younger sisters and one younger brother, and I was only seven! We fought like cats and dogs for attention, affection, and a space in the sun.

Relief came with First Communion. I was to receive God. Despite the two boys down the street, my two sisters and my brother, God would be with me. Communion was proof that God was to be close to me — closer than a heartbeat. But I really wanted more of a sign than Communion at church. Something within me said, "Ask God for a sign. Ask him for a sign even beyond your First Communion." And so I did. I prayed as only a seven-year-old can pray. "God," I said, "if you really are on my side in all these wars around me, give me this sign — let me see a Baltimore Oriole in that blossoming plum tree in our backyard tomorrow." That was my prayer the night before my First Communion, as Admiral Nimitz was about to launch into the Battle of the Coral Sea and General Patton was about to engage the "Desert Fox."

The prophet Isaiah also knew the climate of war. His king was under attack. Two kings to the north had asked him to form an alliance with them so they could do battle with the Assyrians sweeping down from the north. Normally these two kings were like the two boys at the end of my street. They really hated Isaiah's king. But they felt they needed him this time, so they proposed an alliance.

Isaiah stood up to his king: "Do not do it," he said. "Sure, it's a critical time. But don't make alliances with your enemies when things start to go badly. Stick to your old loyalties. Stick to your time-tested commitments. Maintain contact with those with whom you have a history of friendship and allegiance." Isaiah's king backed down and did not make an alliance with his enemies.

The two kings to the north didn't like that. They gave notice. They would sweep down on Jerusalem.

Isaiah, hearing the news, took his son to meet the king at the end of the aqueduct of the Upper Pool in Jerusalem. He brought God's Word in these short phrases: "Be careful, keep calm, and don't be afraid." (7:4) Then he added one more Word from the Lord: "Ask for a sign, whether as high as the heavens or as deep as depths of the earth, ask for a sign." The king would not do it.

"I will not ask," he said. "I will not test the Lord."

Isaiah told him, "Even if you will not ask, the Lord will give you a sign anyway. Not a great plague to wipe out your enemy kings. Nor will he stop the Assyrian chariots from rolling over your land. The sign will be this: a young woman shall conceive and bear a child and his name will be 'Immanuel' which means 'God with us.' "

Luther, commenting on this section of Isaiah said,

Behold the great and overflowing goodness of God and His sublime patience. For even though disdained in His promise and threat, He still does not stop inciting to faith, as if to say: 'if you do not want to believe promises and threats, at least believe the signs and choose whatever you wish.'
(LW 16, 83)

God is always inciting us to faith. When I was seven, he used those two boys down the street so I would turn to him to ask for a sign. God even made use of the battles I had with my sisters and brother over space and time in our household so that I would kneel down that night to seek a sign.

Often, in difficult circumstances, when we feel we are under attack, we are tempted to make alliances with those who really do not have our best interests at heart — that's the time to look for a sign of God's will.

Let it be a simple sign, not something hostile and destructive, like the annihilation of our enemies or a plague on the boys down the street. Let it be simple, like the birth of a child, or an Oriole in a plum tree. Let it be something to reassure us that God is with us, Immanuel.

What happened that First Communion day for me? Did the boys down the street go away? No, they were still there, just waiting for me to take off my white First Communion suit and dare to walk by their homes. Did my brother and sisters stop fighting with me? Are you kidding? But that afternoon, that bright sunny spring day, when I walked into our backyard, there chirping away in our plum tree was the brightest, blackest, orangest Oriole I've ever seen. I knew that God was **Immanuel — God with me. My Communion was complete.**

Isaiah 9:2-7　　　　　　　　　　　The Nativity of Our Lord

The Glance of God

About four hundred years before Jesus was born in Bethlehem, the philosopher Aristotle walked in the Acropolis above Athens. The purpose of life, he said, was to develop one's potential and live up to what was in the human soul, the mind, and the powers of reason.

After him came the philosopher Zeno, a Cypriot, who taught that the aim of life was to avoid all feeling. Virtue stood in the middle, and no extremes of hot anger or cold contempt were to be allowed. His philosophy really caught people's hearts and minds. God glanced at those sun-drenched teachers and said, "No, they have it wrong. I will have to do something. They are not learning it right."

Over on the other side of the world, the priests of Zoroaster were teaching that there were two gods: a god of darkness and a god of light. They developed a finely-tuned ethical system to placate the god of darkness and stave off the god of light. The Lord God glanced their way and said, "They have missed it, too. I will have to do something spectacular, for they still are not getting it right."

Then the Lord shifted his glance towards Israel, his chosen people. Centuries before, their ancestor Abraham had been told to leave his home and his father, and go to a new land. Abraham, hoping against hope, believed what the Lord had said and left Ur of the Chaldeans for the Promised Land.

The chosen people had wandered off the mark. Worshiping golden calves or hurling their children to gods called Baal, they tried to win God's favor. Believing in their own potential to control God, they tried to be perfect in his presence.

So the Lord God of Israel stared at his people. With a long, hard look, he raised up the prophet Isaiah. "The Lord God says your potential is like that of grass," said Isaiah, "to wither in the heat of the sun, and your potential is like that of the flower, to fade away after a few days of glory. But the Word of the Lord stands forever!" (40:6-8) This fiery prophet taught God's people that their only potential was in the Word of the Lord. Their minds, hearts, or power of reason were nothing. Their potential was in God.

To teach them this lesson, the Lord brought the Assyrians up the Euphrates and down the desert to ransack the cities of Israel. When the king said, "O, woe is me and woe is us," he felt only despair in his heart. At that point the Lord said, "A young woman shall bear a child, and his name shall be Immanuel, God with us . . . (7:14) He shall be called Wonderful Counselor, Everlasting Father, Mighty God, and Prince of Peace." What potential! And it was all from God!

The first one born after those prophecies was Hezekiah. After him came others, like Ezra and Nehemiah and Judas Maccabaeus, but God's gaze did not fix on them. His long, hard look finally focused on a woman named Mary and a man named Joseph of the house of David. His eye stopped over a manger in Bethlehem where God's Word was made flesh and dwelt among us.

This was God's spectacular glance our way. This glance sent his Son into our flesh, not to do away with our weakness and frailty, but to give hope as we feel the withering come on or to give courage as we feel the fading begin. Pope Leo the Great, who stood outside Rome in the 300s of our era to confront Attila the Hun and send that ravager back to the Danube, preached the first great Christmas sermon. He said, "The Word of God became flesh . . . Majesty took on humility; strength, weakness; and eternity took on mortality." (Sermon 21, 2)

When that Child was born in Bethlehem, he was weak as

we all are weak, but the strength of God rested in his flesh. Death knocked at the door of the manger, yet the power of God to raise Jesus from the dead shone more brilliantly than that death, like the star in the sky. The Child was born humble, of the earth. His flesh and blood were made of the same stuff as ours, but the majesty of God protected him with a glance that never left his side. This same majesty watches over and protects us.

God never said to his son, "Jesus, you are loaded with potential, so live up to it." No, he said, "You are my Son, in you I am well pleased." "I have sent you to gather together the lost sheep of Israel, and I have anointed you with the spirit of wisdom and understanding so that you may bind up the broken-hearted and bring light to the blind and let the crippled walk."

I have never been to Bethlehem at Christmas or at any other time. If I ever am there, I hope I will come with a sense of how blind, crippled, and broken-hearted I am without God. I hope, too, that I will reach out like a child for the light, power, and healing of God. Children love to reach for things. That is why, I think, the Word became flesh not in a thirty-three-year-old carpenter-teacher named Jesus, but in an infant. God's first human gesture was to reach for someone he needed.

Our potential by birth is not great, it is only trouble, anxiety, and death. God's potential, as he looks our way, is beyond greatness — life, freedom, and healing. In the birth of Christ, we are born to life, healing, and freedom. Apart from his birth, we are born only to death, injury, and despair. His birth becomes ours only by faith. God's eternal glance in our direction opens us when we are shut down with inertia and illumines me when I prefer to be in the dark. By this gift of faith, our hearts are opened to receive his undying loyalty.

This Christmas, may the birth of our Lord Jesus give us a new sense of his peace precisely where we feel at war. May God's long, loyal glance our way give us the strength to say: "Lord, we do believe. We believe you are our Wonderful Counselor, our Everlasting Father, our Eternal God, our Prince of Peace."

Isaiah 63:7-9   *Christmas 1*

Burning Torches

My friend, Bob, recently bought a wood stove. It gives out that thick wrap-around heat which only such stoves can give. How he loves his stove, basking in the comfort and warmth which were not there before. Of course, he has to clean out the ashes every once in a while. If he doesn't, no air circulates from beneath to keep the fire going.

One day he took out half a bucket of ashes and threw them in a trash can outside his house. That night a strong wind blew up the creek, stirring the ashes. About two o'clock in the morning Bob smelled smoke, the stench of burning trash. He ran to the window to see his trash can in flames. How could that be? Who had set the fire? He put the fire out and then sat down to figure out what had happened. No one had set that fire except himself. He had not noticed, but when he shoveled those ashes from his wood stove, the cinders were not all dead. They were not glowing red, except inside where he could not see them. The strong wind fanned the heat to the surface where it ignited the trash in the barrel — and that is how his trash barrel became a burning torch at two o'clock in the morning.

God is often like that in our lives, too, a hidden cinder, still glowing inside the wood, invisible until the Spirit fans the ember to flame.

When the prophet Isaiah said, "I will recount the steadfast love of the Lord, the praises of the Lord, according to all the Lord has granted us," he felt God in his heart like the sun about to burst over the horizon or an ember about to explode into flame.

What was going on in his time that he experienced God that way? While in exile in Babylon, he had gathered with his fellow Jews each Sabbath to read about Moses, Abraham, Isaac, and Joseph. It seems to me that Joseph especially intrigued him. Sold by his brothers into slavery in Egypt, Joseph had smoldered like a quiet cinder for years until God's Spirit finally burst him into flames as the Pharaoh's chief steward.

Like Joseph, the writer of this passage knew the crucible of exile. There he had experienced God's Spirit fanning him to new prophetic life. Then God had led him home.

When the people returned to Jerusalem, the city was in ruins. Into that rubble heap the prophet threw the cinder of God's Word. He preached a message of hope when hope was not to be seen. Where destruction lay all around, he cried out, "I will tell of the kindness of the Lord, the deeds for which He is to be praised." Those deeds included the creation of the world, when God's tempest fanned the coals of human clay to life. They included the wars that God had sent to put down the kings who thought they were unfellable timbers. They encompassed even the Exile when the Lord, brushing their tongues with a taste of desert, also gave his people a thirst for the living Word.

In our personal lives God often lets us lie like dead coals so he can send his Spirit to fan his presence into flames in our lives.

Seven years ago I was just beginning a part-time internship at Ascension Lutheran Church in Baltimore. Since my future was so unclear, my life felt like a burnt-out coal. But even then God's Spirit was fanning me to new life as a steward of his Word. Luther had the same experience in his day. Shortly before he lectured on this part of the Prophet Isaiah, he had met with a small group of men like himself, all reformers in the Church. One of them, Ulrich Zwingli, came from Zurich. At the meeting in the castle of Philip of Hesse in Marburg, they discussed the meaning of the Lord's Supper. Zwingli said it was a symbol of God's presence. Luther said God was truly there for us. Their arguments bounced back and forth for days until Luther took a piece of chalk and wrote in bold letters on the table top, "This is my body." That was the end of his argument. Luther had enough of Spirit-less debate.

Why was Luther this bold? He believed that God was the hidden life-giver in all experiences of death, shame, and affliction. "When I feel death, shame, and affliction," he wrote, "I must believe that God is the life-giver and the one who gives favorable testimony. When I feel afflictions, I must believe that God is not afflicting me." (LW 17, 357)

If death comes into my life, God is hidden there. The Spirit will fan that presence to a flame lit for me. When shame buries me, God will bring light and heat for me from that tomb. Whenever I sense affliction close by, God is sending the Spirit, sometimes like a tempest, sometimes like a soft, still breeze, to fan that ember of faith to a burning torch.

Mr. Spock, in *Star Trek IV*, stood before the computer and could not answer the question, "How do you feel?" He had no frame of reference for the answer. There is no spark of feeling in Spock's Vulcan ancestry. For him to answer that question, God must blow his Spirit Spock's way to fan his dead embers to a burning torch. When God's spirit breathes on dry clay, creation begins. Without his Spirit, there is no life at all.

Let us give thanks to God, so often hidden in the embers of death, shame or affliction, and pray that his Spirit will fan those embers to bright and blazing torches according to his steadfast love.

Jeremiah 31:7-14 *Christmas 2*

Tears in Ramah

In my first year in seminary in Washington, D.C., I visited the Embassy of the Lithuanian Government in Exile. This government has not existed in Lithuania since 1940, when the Soviets invaded ostensibly to save that land from German invasion. In fact, however, Stalin had something else in mind. It was called degentrification, transporting masses of people from their homeland to another section of the Soviet Union, and then bringing other peoples, also degentrified, to settle in that land.

I remember listening with startled ears as a tall, thin man with an accent told us of what had happened to his country. I had never heard of such a thing. Deportation is another name for it, or exile. The feeling is dislocation, being cut off, separated. I was twenty-one or twenty-two when I heard about this, and I had a hard time believing that such a thing could really occur. I had not learned about it in my history books.

Since then, however, I have learned that not only nations, but individuals suffer dislocation, and exile. I can still see the boxcars filled with exiled men and women in the movie, *Dr. Zhivago*, and I can still picture refugees streaming from eastern Europe after World War II. Only when exile is very personal does it have intense meaning.

I have felt personal exile three times in my life. Once when I left Minnesota for the seminary, once when I lived in France, and once when I became a Lutheran. I left Minnesota for seminary in Baltimore, Maryland, when I was nineteen. I had never lived in a large city before, with three major railroad stations, rows and rows of brick houses, and ships anchored in the harbor. God had a purpose in that exile. I was to learn how to live in an urban world. In France, I learned to live in another culture. When I became a Lutheran, God taught me to live in another religious tradition.

Only from reading and meditating on the Old Testament have I come to appreciate how God acts when we are in these exile experiences. We all have them. When a friend dies or goes away, we feel loss. When a job ends or a career changes, we feel dislocation. When young people leave home for college or career, they feel exiled. There is no living without exile.

That is where the Old Testament and God's gift of faith come in. In the days of the Prophet Jeremiah, God sent warning after warning to his people that Exile was coming. It had to. God had a purpose in sending it. Jeremiah was just a young man when he stood up in Jerusalem to warn of the deportation to come. Later on, he described it this way: "A voice is heard in Ramah, lamentation and bitter weeping. Rachel is weeping for her children, because they are not." At Ramah, a transition point from Jerusalem to Babylon, the exiles stopped to live as strangers in a strange land. Rachel, of course, was long dead at that time, but Jeremiah portrayed her as weeping from her grave over her children who were torn from their land.

Then the prophet raised his voice again:

Thus says the Lord: "Keep your voice from weeping and your eyes from tears, for your work shall be rewarded . . . there is hope for you, and your children shall return to their own country . . . with supplications I will lead them back, and I will make them walk by brooks of water, in a straight path in which they shall not stumble . . . for I am a father to Israel, and Ephraim is my first-born."

When we feel exile in our hearts, God has not abandoned us. When we feel lamentation and bitter weeping, as Rachel felt for her children, God is still with us. When we feel we do not even want to be comforted, God then sends his word: "There is hope for you . . . He who scattered you will gather you and will keep you as a shepherd keeps his flock." Exile tests faith.

Luther felt this. He felt it strongly in his forty-seventh year. The Emperor had convened the Diet of Augsburg attempting to force the Protestants to recant. Luther was advised by his Prince not to go to Augsburg for this Imperial Convocation, so he stayed in exile in Coburg, three day's distance away. There was lamentation and bitter weeping in his heart as he received reports of how badly things were going. He may have felt the urge to refuse to be comforted. Then one evening, in a blaze of faith, as though the sun had burst through his dark clouds of loss, he grabbed a piece of charcoal and wrote on the wall of his study this verse from Psalm 118: "I shall not die, but live, and declare the works of the Lord."

The time of exile turned out to be a time for special productivity for Luther, as it was for the prophets of Israel and as it always has been for me. Luther translated the Hebrew prophets into German during this time. He also wrote many letters, one of them an especially poignant message to his young son, Hans.

In exile God also gave Luther the crystalization of his thoughts about his personal seal, a black cross in a red heart, set in a white rose. That white rose blossoms in a blue sky, circled by a golden ring. Luther wrote that although God's cross hurts us, it never destroys. The black of the cross was to represent mortification. The rose symbolizes faith, keeping our hearts alive in joy. The blue stands for the joy of heaven as we walk through Christ's cross to the golden ring of blessedness without end.

Luther's seal has helped me when I have felt exile, loss, or exclusion. It is a prophet's seal, a constant reminder that God scatters and then gathers again. He is our Father whose loyalty turns our exiles into entrances into his promised land. He is the hope of our future who wipes away every tear from our eyes.

Isaiah 60:1-6   Epiphany

Who are these Kings?

Just before Christmas one year, I took our three-year-old nursery school class on a tour of the church, to tell them the story of Christmas. The Christmas window with the Three Kings, Mary, and Jesus is a nursery school favorite. I asked the class who the baby was. "Jesus," one little girl replied. "Who is the lady carrying him in her arms?" "That's his Mother." "What's her name?" No one knew. Finally another little girl said, "Mary." Then I asked them, "And who are these three men?" A long silence followed. Finally a bright, black-haired boy said, "Those are his grandparents!"

Who are these kings?

If you travel to the Cathedral of Cologne, on the Rhine River in Germany, you will find, in an enameled shrine, the purported remains of these kings with a description of their deaths. It reads as follows:

Having undergone many trials and fatigues for the Gospel, the Three Wise Men met at Seqwa (Sebate in Armenia) in 54 A.D. to celebrate the feast of Christmas. Thereupon, after the celebration of the Mass, they died: St. Melchior on January 1st, aged 116; St. Balthsasaar on January 6th, aged 112; and St. Gaspar on January 11th, aged 109.

Those names appear nowhere in the Bible. In fact, they don't appear anywhere much before the sixth century.

So, who are these kings?

We must first take a look at the Old Testament lesson from the Prophet Isaiah to discover their purpose and then ask: "What do they mean for us?" Primarily they are men of faith. Matthew does not call them kings at all, but "Magi" from the east.

When the Prophet Isaiah spoke of "caravans of camels covering your land and bringing gold and frankincense," his real point was that those bringing that gold and frankincense came to praise the Lord God of Israel. Isaiah was speaking to Jews returned to Jerusalem after their Exile in Babylon. The Persian Emperor, Artaxerxes, was making Jerusalem one of Persia's temple-fortress cities. Taxes had been levied on the peoples of Sheba, Media, and other parts of Arabia to bring their gold, frankincense, lumber, carpenters, rocks and stone masons to build the temple of the Lord in Jerusalem.

Isaiah looked at historical fact with the eyes of faith. He interpreted this decree of the Persian Emperor as the end of dark times for Israel and for the world. God would no longer allow a shadowy cloud of exile to remain over his people. He would be sunlight for their darkness. This decree was not just a clever military strategy on the Persian's part, said Isaiah. This was the Lord God of Israel rebuilding Jerusalem and the temple so that all nations could worship there. All peoples would now share in the mercy, kindness, and steadfast love of God the Lord God of Israel . . . even the Magi.

When Saint Matthew wrote his Gospel, five hundred years after Isaiah's prophecy, he remembered what the prophet had said. He believed that Jesus was the brightest light God would ever send to the earth. Matthew brought to his Gospel story the same theme that Isaiah had woven in his prophecy: The Lord God of Israel would break away the clouds of doom and the storms of despair that shrouded all peoples. Only Matthew reports the story of the Magi from the east. They are crucial to the theme of his entire Gospel: In Jesus God has been revealed for all people. In Jesus we are all born to new life and to the new light of hope in the midst of our cloudiest days.

The Magi came as men of faith from the east. As Magi they were probably priests of the religion of Zoroaster, astrologers who lived by the signs of the Zodiac. Was one a Capricorn, one a Sagittarius, one a Scorpio? We don't know. We know only that they were Magi from the east. Their names, their ages when they died, and where they are buried, are not really that important. What is important is that they left all to do homage to their king. They followed his star, not their own, and they let the light of God's dawn break through their darkness. They had lived under a cloud for a long time. When the time was right, they walked from that cloud to the brilliance of God's new dawn in their lives.

About twenty-five years ago, I stood in the airport in Teheran at four a.m. I wanted to step out on the runway to see the sky those Magi had scanned. In that part of the world the night sky is like an inverted bowl of black ink and the stars dance like diamonds in the liquid sky. I began to understand more about those wise men who studied the stars for thousands of years there, those Magi. I also began to understand how they must have appreciated the dawn, for the night is thick there. The darkness does not just cover you, it fills you, and you begin to think that all real life is in that inky sky. So taught the astrologers, the Magi. These three left that darkness for God's undying light. They came on their camels, bringing gold, frankincense, and myrrh to praise the Lord God of Israel. For the glory of the Lord had arisen upon them and they streamed to Bethlehem to see the light made flesh in the Child.

They did not come as astrologers. They came to Bethlehem as men of faith, part of God's new dayspring for the world. Nor did they arrive just with fire, the usual travel gift of the priests of Zoroaster in those days. They brought gold, frankincense, and myrrh. Luther had something to say about their gifts: The gold signifies their faith in Jesus as their king; the frankincense, that he was their priest; and the myrrh, that he would die for them.

Sometimes God will leave us in darkness for a long, long time. Like the Magi, we will search that darkness for signs of life and hope. In that search, God is preparing us to be ready to move when his dawn comes our way. Then he will seal his blazing imprint on our poor clay and dye our faded garments with his own brilliant hues.

Isaiah 42:1-9   **The Baptism of Our Lord**

Given as Light

A young man sat near a small river, his feet cooling in the gently rippling water. He had walked many miles that day through the desert dust. The river soothed him and calmed the restless longing in his soul. He was almost thirty years old. As he grew up in his father's carpenter shop, his kinsfolk thought he would be a carpenter, too. But he left one day, never to return, to become a teacher, a wandering rabbi calling men and women to follow him.

As he sat there on the banks of the shallow river, another man appeared, walking in the river. A craggy, stick-iron man, he fixed his fiery eyes on the man by the shore. "Behold the Lamb of God," he cried, "Behold him who takes away the sin of the world." (John 1:29)

John the Baptizer startled Jesus. Jesus had no followers at this time. He was alone. But he did have a sense, deep in his heart, that something lay in store for him, perhaps something he had discovered in his meditation on the prophet Isaiah.

Jesus took very literally the words from Isaiah: "Behold my servant whom I uphold, my chosen, in whom my soul delights." Perhaps, as with other young people, Jesus sometimes felt that God had forgotten him. Perhaps he felt the desperate need for friendship that adolescents feel. These words from Isaiah could console and strengthen him: "Behold my servant, whom I uphold, my chosen, in whom my soul delights."

No matter how isolated he might feel, Jesus was God's chosen one. Upheld by God no matter what, he was the one in whom God delighted.

I remember talking with a friend as we were leaving high school for college. We asked each other what we feared most about this transition. My friend, who later became an attorney in Arizona, said, "I'm most afraid of losing my friends."

Did Jesus have such a fear? He always treated his friends very candidly and directly. "Get thee behind me, Satan," he said to Peter, when Peter rejected his talk of cross and resurrection. At the Last Supper, as he girded himself with towel and washed the feet of his closest friends, did he fear they would run away?

Even when Judas betrayed him with a kiss, Jesus held out the hand of friendship. Because he had in his heart this Word of God from Isaiah, Jesus could withstand even betrayers like Judas: "Behold my servant whom I uphold, my chosen one, in whom my soul delights."

Yet another Word of God could support Jesus as he sat by the River Jordan the day John the Baptizer came along. His feet bathing in the ripples, Jesus may have felt these words from Isaiah sear his heart like a branding iron, "I have called you in righteousness. I have taken you by the hand and kept you. I have given you as a covenant to the people and as a light to the nations." God would work through this man.

Later when his kinsfolk said he was crazy and his townsfolk tried to kill him, Jesus continued his work, trusting God. When they nailed him to the Cross, he believed that Cross could light up the nations.

Even though this prophecy refers first and foremost to Jesus of Nazareth, it also applies to each of us *through him* as well. We are all a little like my friend in high school who feared the loss of his friends. We all have our fears. We all have our attacks of loneliness. And we all have problems in our families. That is how life is. Jesus knew that. He learned it by experience. He also had the prophet Isaiah and the Word of God written there as a great source of strength and consolation in his life. "I have taken you by the hand and have kept you . . . I have given you as a covenant to the people, a light to the nations."

When the prophet first spoke these words, he was a long way from the River Jordan and a long way from Jerusalem. He, with many of his fellow Jews, was in Exile in Babylon on the Euphrates River, in modern day Iraq. Word from God gave them hope in what looked like a hopeless situation and light in a darkened land. The promise was this: Even though you are far from home, God still delights in you. He still takes you by the hand. He will make you a light for all nations.

Luther, like Isaiah, felt called by God to give light to the world. Had he actually visited many of the lands where his words were heard and his books were read, he would have been burned at the stake as a heretic. "Apart from Christ," he said, "there is nothing but darkness and dungeon. Who can always believe that, when we seem to be seeing and in paradise? . . . All lights apart from Christ are darkness, as is free will." (LW 17, 69)

Even when we feel the darkness inside, the light of Christ is there. Even when we feel in Exile, God calls us home. When we feel brokenness in our villages or families, God moves us through those experiences to his Word. God's Word will not break the bruised reed, nor will it quench the dimly burning wick. He will light the wick in our hearts to illuminate our darkness and transform our fears to brilliant hope.

Isaiah 49:1-7   Epiphany 2

Hid in God

One hot day in August I was sitting in the chaplain's office at the Georgia Regional Hospital outside of Atlanta, watching the sun's long, warm rays crawl across the hospital grounds, when the phone rang. I picked it up. A nurse from the admissions unit told me, "Chaplain, Nancy has run away again, can you come down here?" "Sure," I said, "I'll be right down." "Please hurry," she said. "All the male attendants have left and we don't think any of us can catch her." I drove quickly to the admissions building, about a half-mile away.

The admissions building always had an eerie feel about it. The lighting was indirect and diffused softly, supposedly to keep down anxiety. I found it depressing. I began to wonder if Nancy did, too. Maybe that was why she ran away so much. The head nurse, a feisty woman from north Georgia in her late forties, organized us in teams of two to begin the search. As we left the building, one of the patients, a good friend of Nancy's, waved to me. "Hello, Chaplain," she said.

I found Nancy sitting behind a tree. As the other staff person searching with me reached us, Nancy looked at me and said, "What's the use?" I paused to ask God for an answer. No answer came, so I said, "How should I know?"

Nancy was an ex-nun, now a patient in a mental hospital. I was still a Catholic priest, then a chaplain in that same hospital.

When we returned to the admissions unit, the head nurse

locked Nancy in a solitary room — for punishment, I guess. I sat down in one of the chairs near Nancy's friend.

"Chaplain," she said, "it's no good to put Nancy in the solitary room." "I agree," I said, "but it's not my decision." "They all think she runs away," she went on. "Oh?" I said. "Say some more." "She runs away to get caught — especially by you . . . she runs away to get caught."

"Thank you," I replied, stunned. That mentally ill patient helped me to see what was really going on. She helped me to see that so often in our lives we all do the same thing. There is a little Nancy in each of us — a little run-away or a little hide-away. We like to run away — not just to run away, but so we can be caught. We like to hide — not just to hide, but so we can be found to prove we are not forgotten. That's why "Hide and Seek" is such a popular game with children.

The people of Israel stood on the banks of the Euphrates River in Babylon wondering why their ancestors had been carried off from Jerusalem. Why had they been hidden away in Babylon? They wondered if God had forgotten them.

Isaiah's reply was that they were not forgotten. God was with them. They had needed a period of hiding, and they had needed a period of running away. Why? So they could be found and so they could be caught. God had hidden them away until the appropriate time.

Isaiah went on. "Listen to me," he said. "The Lord God called me from the womb, from the body of my mother he named me. He made my mouth like a sharp sword, in the shadow of his hand he hid me."

That's a great image for our lost and forgotten feelings: "In the shadow of his hand, God hides me." We need that time of hiddenness, as protection and preparation. And we need faith in such times that God will bring us out again.

The Prodigal Son ran away and hid himself in a pig sty so his father could find him again. I felt hidden for many years as a seminary professor. I was so comfortable hiding behind those big stone walls. Oh it was a little depressing and a little boring at times, but even boredom and isolation can become comfortable after a while.

Then, one day in August, Fr. Americo Di Norcia in Gaithersburg, Maryland, called because he needed someone to preach on Sundays. And I agreed to do it. I really liked it. And the people liked me.

I began to wonder, "Has God been hiding me at St. Paul's College until Gaithersburg needed me?" Later on I asked, "Has he been hiding me here in the Paulist Fathers so he could find me as a Lutheran?"

The prophet Isaiah continued to speak about his "hidden away" feelings: "He made me a polished arrow and then in his quiver he hid me away."

When God is preparing us for work, polishing us, sharpening our points, and putting nice feathers on us, we think, "He's about to shoot me forward into life!" Then what happens? He sticks us in his quiver for a month or a year or a decade or four decades. Only then does he pull us out, string the bow, and say, "Now, I'm ready for you. I'm ready to shoot you to the mark."

While we are in God's quiver, so nicely polished, pointed and feathered, we may feel like things are not going well for us. Isaiah felt that: "But I thought," he said, "I have labored in vain, spent my strength for nothing." God has a purpose for those feelings and those times in our lives: to get us to rely on him and not on our high polish, sharp points or fine feathers. It is God, after all, who shoots the arrow to the mark.

Luther certainly had his quiver years. God polished, pointed and feathered him for a long time in the monastery where he gave him great powers of speech, thought, administration and leadership. For many years this was all hidden away. When God finally put Luther in the bow and pulled the string, that arrow sped around the world. It is still speeding today in those of us who call ourselves Christians.

God taught Luther many things in those quieter years, just

as he does when he takes us apart from time to time. He hides us so we can be sharpened and polished, prepared for the task. But do not be deceived. This quiet time is not a permanent arrangement. None of our arrangements are. It is only temporary, as all God's arrangements for us are. If we are hidden away with God for a while, we will be shot into the fray once again. God will see to that.

In quiver times, when I feel I am hidden away, God is still my sovereign. His claim is still on me. His demand that I be his and his alone still stands. "I was precious in the sight of God, and the Lord was my strength," said Isaiah.

God hides us away sometimes so we can feel as Isaiah, Jesus, and Luther felt in their quiver years. He leads us to cry out, "Lord, now I see . . . yes, I am precious in your sight, and you are my strength. I am in your hands."

Isaiah 9:1-4 *Epiphany 3*

Wait and Hope

Damascus was important to both Isaiah and Paul. For both, it was the city of the enemy, the place where the danger dwelt — not so much physical danger, but danger to their very souls and identities.

For Isaiah, seven hundred years before Jesus, Damascus housed King Rezin, who sought to have Isaiah's King join forces with him. "Together," said Rezin, "we can defeat the armies from the East."

For Paul of Tarsus, Damascus housed the Christians, those followers of the Way, prompting so many of Paul's friends to abandon the Law and the Temple as the bed-rock of their religious identity.

Two men on fire. Two men on fire because of faith. Two men aflame with a passion for the living God.

God has different ways of dealing with such people. God took Isaiah to the temple in a vision and purified his lips with a burning coal so that he could preach for God. God prompted him to say: "Here am I, Lord! Send me!" (6:8)

Saul of Tarsus had to be blinded and turned around. God sent a flash of light from heaven so he would fall on his knees to ask: "Lord, what would you have me to do?"

God deals strongly and roughly with his friends, because God knows how resistant and rebellious we are. God does not like to spend time with passive animals comfortable in their own dust. Should we slide into that restful ash heap, we can count on God's Word coming like coal-fire to burn our lips so we can say, "Here I am, Lord. Send me." God will surround us with his blinding light until *we* fall to our knees to say, "Lord, what wilt *thou* have *me* to do?"

Nothing stung these two men more than their compatriots' snug ease. They in turn found Isaiah and Paul painfully disturbing. Isaiah's contemporaries began to run like little prairie dogs throughout Jerusalem, crying out, "To the testimony and to the Law." "Keep the law and honor the King," they meant. "Don't listen to this mad prophet Isaiah with his spectacles of gloom."

To his prairie dog companions, Isaiah cried out, I will not anchor my life on the King, nor will I present to the Lord how well I keep the law. "I will wait for the Lord, even when he hides his face, and I will hope in him." (8:17)

Paul's contemporaries once pummeled him with stones until he was half dead. Many years later Paul wrote, "I count everything as loss for the high privilege of knowing Christ Jesus my Lord." (Philippians 3:8)

Both Isaiah and Paul had been raised with their flesh steeped in belief in God's strength. God's zeal, they believed, smote thousands with a glance; he won battles and divided the spoil.

But God had other shows of strength as well, when he burned Isaiah's lips with a coal or blinded Saul with his brilliant light. God was also strong as Immanuel, Who walked with Adam in the cool of the evening. To Immanuel Jesus prayed in the Garden of Gethsemane, "Father, let this cup pass from me . . . yet not my will, but yours be done." Immanuel . . . the God who is close by, no matter what.

After Isaiah had said, "I will wait and hope, even though God hides his face from me now," his opponents scurried to their precious Law and their precious king. They launched a final glorious protest to this burning man. "No more gloom," they said. "No more darkness . . . for to us a child shall be born, and he shall be called Wonderful Counselor, Everlasting

Father, and Prince of Peace. We will have another Solomon and another David on the throne. The zeal of the Lord of Hosts will do this." Though they had misunderstood the message, they had begun to hope for salvation.

Centuries after Isaiah, those Christians who dwelt in Damascus read his words and they tasted like honey in their mouths. As God touched their lips and blinded them with his light, they came to understand that this Wonderful Counselor and Prince of Peace was not another David or another Solomon in his glory, but an obscure carpenter's son who had been crucified by the Romans and raised from the dead by God.

This was the group that had so enraged Saul that he wanted to put them all into chains to kill them. Instead, they took this blinded lion in. One of them said, "Brother Saul, the Lord Jesus who appeared to you on the road by which you came has sent me that you may regain your sight and be filled with the Holy Spirit." (Acts 9:17)

God has his burning coal for each of our lips. When we feel like shriveling up and lying at ease in our ashes, he ignites us so we will stand up to say, "Here am I, Lord. Send me." He has his blinding light for each of us, just as we are on our way to destroy someone whom God has sent to challenge our stiff-necked ways. God's brilliance helps us say once again, "Lord, what wilt *thou* have me to do?"

This God who burns and blinds our foolish ways is the God who walks with us in the cool of the evening. Count on it — he will hide his face in our lives so we can wait and hope in him.

Micah 6:1-8   Epiphany 4

Micah's Orders

On Baltimore's near West Side, there is a winding hilly way which may have been a deer trail long before the Europeans settled in this land. Along that road stands a fine grey stone fortress, with a steeple stretching to the stars. In 1875, the members of First English Lutheran Church, who had been burned out of their church home on Park Avenue, built that fortress.

I was near there a few weeks ago, returning from a visit with one of our members who worshiped in that church as a girl.

From a stop light, I saw the old church off to my right, just two blocks away. At one time this had been a highly fashionable and comfortable place to live. Many of those homes once had polished wooden stairways at both the front and the back doors. The neighborhood is run down now. It is sad to see. Trash litters the alley behind what once was the parsonage, and the glass door into the church is chained shut.

Still, the fortress has a majesty, in proud defiance of the surrounding decay. Does it know that even this will pass? On the outside wall hangs a bronze tablet with these words engraved: "New Shiloh Baptist Church."

I knocked on the glass door. A young woman unlocked the chain to let me in. "I'm Pastor Lynch," I said, "from First English Lutheran Church. This church was built as First English Lutheran Church."

"Oh, yes," she said, "I know. We found a note when we

took the organ out." "I'd love to see it," I said. "Fine," she replied, "but it has been remodeled at least twice since it was yours. The stairways are right down there."

I walked through the fellowship hall to climb the winding stairway up to the nave, taking one step at a time. At the top, in the narthex, the old swinging doors stood before me, waiting to be pushed open. I hesitated. What did I expect to find? A former Pastor's ghost? An old Lutheran organ pipe? A long since played melody from Bach? What I did find was an enormous arched chamber, like the inside of a giant bell. Around the walls at the top, painted into the plaster were the Beatitudes, "Blessed are the poor in Spirit . . . Blessed are the meek . . . Blessed are those who hunger and thirst after justice."

Where the altar once stood were choir benches, with the pulpit front and center. On the back wall of the chancel was stretched a mural of a black man in a large wheat field with the bold words: "My strength is in the Lord."

None of this, though, struck me as much as the brass plaque in the undercroft honoring the former pastors: Only three names are there, but under their names is written, "Do justice, love mercy, and walk humbly with thy God." (Micah 6:8) What a tribute, I thought. This church honors its pastors not for the members brought in, or balanced budgets achieved. They are not honored for anything except that they did justice, loved mercy, and walked humbly with their God.

As a Pastor, I knew that nothing would please me more than those three things. As a Pastor? As a Christian! As a child of the God who alone is just and who walks with his children in the cool of the evening.

The prophet Micah came from a run-down neighborhood, too. Unlike his contemporary Isaiah, who may have been an aristocrat with easy access to the king, Micah came from the countryside. He left his vegetables and lambs behind to bring a better commodity: God's Word. Jerusalem was not loving mercy, doing justice, or walking humbly with their God. So Micah stood up in the city and said, "Arise, and quarrel with God . . . plead your case before him."

Micah, like all the prophets, never encouraged anyone to lie down and sleep in the presence of the living God. He wanted people up on their feet, arguing with the Lord. Micah dared them to defend themselves before the throne of God. Micah, more than all the others, exposed the cozy feeling God's people had developed because of their fine temple and elegant ritual. God, they thought, was locked in the ark of the Covenant to do their bidding. They leaned on God, said this bucolic prophet, and the day was coming when "Jerusalem shall become a heap of ruins and Zion shall be plowed as a field."

Too much in torpor because of their princely temple, God's people had fallen into the decay that eats at all religious people who trim up their churches and forget to "do justice." What does that mean, to "do justice?"

The word in Hebrew for "justice" is "mishpot." It means, "Who is my judge?" "Who is my Lord?" "Who exercises sovereignty over me?" To "do justice" means to act, quarrel, walk, and pray in such a way that I constantly affirm that God is my judge, my Lord, and the sovereign in my life. Only that One exercises Lordship over me. I serve no other Master.

Luther's keen awareness of God's Lordship in his life gushed to the surface in his *Small Catechism*, written after he had heard of beer recipes passing for sermons during his visitation of the parish churches near Wittenberg. In his commentary on the Second Article of the Apostles' Creed he wrote:

> *I believe that Jesus Christ, true God, begotten of the Father from eternity, and also true man, born of the Virgin Mary, is my Lord, who has redeemed me . . . delivered me and freed me . . . in order that I may be his own, live under him in his kingdom and serve him in everlasting righteousness, innocence, and blessedness, even as he is risen from the dead and lives and reigns to all eternity.*

Luther believed he stood under the judgment of the Lord who loved him. Nothing mattered more in his life. This belief kept him restless for God.

Did the pastors at New Shiloh Baptist church face a congregation growing cozy in their beautiful new building? Did they "do justice and love mercy and walk humbly before their God" because their congregation was in danger of falling into temple worship, the idolatry of stone, glass, and polished wood? Or did these pastors, in their own lives, merely reflect the lives of their people, who refused to worship brick, mortar and bits of colored glass? In fact, has New Shiloh long been a place where Jesus is Lord?

In that mural behind the choir, way down in the corner, is a tiny painting of a bright new church. I asked about it. New Shiloh is moving. Their time at Lanvale and Freemont Streets is over.

"What will you do with this building?" I asked.

"We will sell it," she replied.

I don't know who will buy it, and I don't know what it will be used for — but I do know this. I have a hope for that building, built in 1875, sold in 1925, and now about to be sold again. I hope it will continue to stand as a witness to what the prophet Micah said. May it continue to prod people who want to sleep their lives away with the worship of stone and glass to "do justice, love mercy, and walk humby with their God."

Isaiah 58:5-9a   *Epiphany 5*

What God Sees

Salzburg is a splendid town, rolling in and out of the hills that dance about the Salzer River. In the town center sits a fortress topped with many castles. Below that hill Salzburg's fairyland cathedral stretches its bulging roccoco arms this way and that to offer its praise to the Lord.

I lived in Salzburg a few weeks one summer, studying German at the University. I loved to walk through the town, its narrow streets leading me up secret alleys to hidden surprises. Up one street stood Mozart's birthplace, down another a rosy-cheeked Austrian girl sold milk from a street cart. I was one of her most frequent and steady customers.

In the afternoons our professors guided us through the villages and palaces in the countryside. In the evening I learned German by walking all over the city with a Yugoslavian priest who spoke to me only in German, describing the wonderous beauty of Salzburg.

The most famous palace in the countryside is the former residence of the Prince-Archbishop of Salzburg. Its landscaped gardens seek to reconstruct the garden of Eden. The halls in the palace take one's breath away. Long before Walt Disney's "Imagineers" the prince-archbishop brought in Italian hydraulic engineers to set up fountains with moving puppets and elfin waterfalls. Salzburg's population swells each summer for the Mozart Festival. Musicians arrive from all over the world for this world-class musical event. Salzburg is one of the happiest places I have ever lived.

But it was not always that way. Salzburg is Catholic land. It always has been. For many years its prince was also an archbishop of the Roman Catholic Church. After the Protestant Reformation, however, many Lutherans settled in that area. Life was never too easy for them, depending on the archbishop and his feelings about Lutherans.

In 1727, five years before George Washington was born, Leopold Anthony von Firmian became the ruler of Salzburg. He resolved to rid his principality of its Protestant dissenters. "I would rather have thorns and thistles on my fields," he said, "than Lutherans on my land." To his astonishment, after he introduced repressive measures, 19,000 peasants defiantly registered as adherents of the Augsburg Confession. Leopold's response was arrests, prohibition of meetings, and the suppression of baptisms, marriages, and funerals for Protestants. On Reformation Day, 1731, he gave all Protestants this ultimatum: "Become Catholic or leave."

Thirty thousand persons left. They streamed northward to Germany and England. Some came to the new colony established by James Oglethorpe in America where they set up a Lutheran colony near Savannah, in Ebeneezer, Georgia. Some fled to Leipzig, where Johann Sebastian Bach lived. Leipzig was not to be outdone by the other German cities in welcoming these refugees. So moved by their plight and thus inspired to arouse public sympathy on their behalf, Bach composed a contata based on this lesson from Isaiah.

The *feeling* in this passage is exile, abandonment, and persecution for religious identity and belief. The need is for restoration. Once home, lands, church, and familiar surroundings are no more, asked the prophet, what does God give us to nourish identity, rebuild our homes, and strengthen our religious belief?

Isaiah addressed exiles like those from Salzburg. Isaiah's people had been driven out of Jerusalem in 587 B.C. Then, thanks to Cyrus, King of Persia, they had been sent back home.

When they returned to Jerusalem, the city was in shambles. The Amonites, Moabites, and Edmites had taken over their land.

How were they to re-establish their land? What was the true path of restoration? Many of the leaders said, "The only way to restore it is to have things just the way they were. We must rebuild the temple." Others said, "No, let's be like these people who live here now. Let's compromise with them." They all gave up on God, thinking God had given up on them. Except Isaiah.

No, he said, restoration after exile is not rebuilding old temples. Nor is it compromising with those whose values are so different from our own. Restoration means loosing the chains of injustice. It means breaking that inner bondage that ruptures my friendships and rebels against God. Only God breaks that bondage. Only God restores.

Luther was well aware of those inner enslaving cords. He always maintained that human nature is bound to rebel against the righteousness of God. That rebellion leads to the rupture of social relationships and to inner turmoil and unrest. The remedy, said Luther, is faith. That is where true restoration comes in *all* our lives. He wrote: "This is the true glory of God, when I have proved my faith to believe that God is well disposed toward me and that what I do is not the result of my effort but is by the goodness of God." (LW 17, 288)

However God chooses to break my inner chains and lead me to righteousness, he always is well disposed to me. If I have compassion, it is because God has given it to me. If I can share with others, it is because God has equipped me to do so. If I can come back home after exile, it is because God has brought me safely there.

Deuteronomy 30:15-20   *Epiphany 6*

Daily Choice

One of my earliest childhood sweethearts was, believe it or not, a woman named Sophie Tucker. I have never really figured out why, but something about that woman charmed and fascinated me when I was a child. She used to sing a song called "Life Begins at Forty." One of my great childhood goals was to buy a record of her singing that song. I even found out that she performed in a club in New York, and I began to make plans to get there to see her in person.

    I began to wonder . . . was it she, or that song she sang, that captured my imagination? Was it her style, or the title of her song, that caught me up in the stream? As I neared my fortieth birthday I really began to believe that things were going to be a lot different after forty — better and better in every way. Sophie Tucker was right, I felt. She belonged right up there with the other great prophets — Isaiah, Jeremiah, and Moses.

    Then it came, the big "four-O." The seminary where I had been teaching closed its doors. Suddenly job security was gone. My best friend in the Paulist Fathers told me he was leaving to get married. It seemed the brotherhood in the Paulist Fathers was not that stable either.

    I went to Russia just before my fortieth birthday. When I came back I was so sick I thought I was going to die. Is this the Promised Land, I asked? Is this the place of milk and honey? I heard the voice of Sophie Tucker, tough, gravely, like a longshoreman's rope tying up an ocean liner. "Life begins at forty, all right," I said. Then somebody said, "It's the second forty that are the most difficult."

The ancient Hebrews were just like me. They lived that grand fantasy that after forty, life would be different. They had wandered for forty years through the Sinai Peninsula, sometimes starving, sometimes thirsty, often rebellious, but never settled down. That's not a bad image of what my first forty years were like — lots of hungers, lots of thirsts, and lots of wandering about. After forty years of this kind of existence, I was ready for a Promised Land! So were the ancient Hebrews!

Like me, those ancient nomadic tribes dreamed of a life with no more hunger, thirst, or wandering. They wanted stability without loss or change of any kind. Moses stood up on a high mountain just east of the Jordan, and let his voice ring like a thunderclap across the desert: "Hear O Israel, the Lord your God is One. And you shall love the Lord your God with all your heart and all your strength and all your soul . . . for the Lord is a devouring fire and a jealous God. Remember this, first of all."

Lest the Israelites think that once they entered that Promised Land there would be no more pain, sorrow, or tears to wipe away, Moses went on: "Hear what the Lord says. Look I have set before you life *and* death, blessing *and* curse. Therefore, choose life!"

Why did Moses give this Word of God as his last will and testament to his people? Why did he put that awful burden of choice on them as they stood there straining toward the Jordan, their lips already drinking in the springs of living water on the other side?

Moses knew that in the human heart lies the ultimate fantasy, that once we pass to the other side of forty, fifty, or eighty, there won't be any more choices to make. No more life and death — just life. No more blessing and curse — just blessing. Thomas More called such a place Utopia, from the Greek that means "no place."

No, this side or that side of forty, we still walk the path strewn with choice. The stones of sorrow lie here; the brambles of suffering lie there. We have to negotiate them. Sometimes, after I pray the Lord's Prayer, I say in my heart, "Give us this day our daily *choice* . . . Lord, help me to choose life."

I add that prayer because choosing life is not that easy. I believe that we choose evil spontaneously and willingly. Only God's Spirit saves us from choosing death and curse. Moses' command made us aware of our inner ability to choose life. Such an order leads us to despair of our own power of choice and to seek out help from God. So captive are we to death, that in our friendships, families, and careers our powers of choice are tilted toward destruction, misery, and loss.

God, in sending his Word to be made flesh for us in Jesus of Nazareth, has released us from that captivity. Yet, the powers of evil still tear at us, fighting against the power of God's Word. We are commanded to choose life, but we cannot, unless God helps us. He helped us definitively in the Cross and Resurrection of Jesus. He helps us each day with his Word and Spirit.

May God's Word, enshrined in our hearts at Baptism, continue to lead us on paths of life. May the Spirit continue to breathe in our souls, lest we choose not to breathe at all. In Christ the choice has been made for us — life always new and life eternal.

Isaiah 49:8-13   *Epiphany 7*

Never Forgotten

At the same time Luther was lecturing to the seminary students in Wittenburg on the meaning of the prophet Isaiah in their personal lives, a marriage took place in France that was to have far-reaching impact on the future of the Protestant Reformation. Margaret of Angouleme, sister of King Francis I, married Duke Henry of Navarre, whose family name was Bourbon. Navarre today lies in Spain in the Pyrenees, where the Basques live. I've been there to visit Basque friends of mine. Touring their churches and villages, local townsfolk told me how they remembered the days of the Spanish Civil War in the 1930s, when their friends were machine-gunned to death in local bistros. Yes, they remember; they do not forget.

    The Bourbons come from that part of the world. A thousand years ago, after the king of Castile was crowned, he journeyed by horseback to the sacred city of the Basque people, there to swear guaranties to their independence. The people of Navarre remember that, even today. They do not forget.

    Margaret, although she never left the Catholic church, was a great admirer of Luther. She read his works and encouraged the rise of Protestantism in France. When Calvin feared for his life in Paris, he sought her protection in Angouleme and found safety there. Margaret's Protestant influence passed on to her children and her grandchildren, especially to her grandson Henry, the first Bourbon king of France.

    Henry had been raised a Protestant. Though he gave up

his Protestantism to become king of France, he did not forget his origins or the strong influence of his grandmother. He issued the Edict of Nantes, assuring freedom of worship to Protestants in more than 3,000 castles in the realm, as well as full civil rights and admission to all schools, universities, and hospitals in the land. Henry was a Bourbon from Navarre. He remembered. He did not forget.

This great capacity for memory worked against the Bourbons over the years. By the time of the French Revolution in 1789, Louis XVI sat in the palace making clocks, while the nation dissolved into anarchy at his feet. What had he learned from his forefathers, Henry IV and Louis XIV, the great Bourbon kings of France? As they led him to the guillotine, what did he recall? A saying arose about the Bourbons: "They forget nothing, but they learn nothing."

That's a terrible thing to say about any family or any person. It means good memory is both a blessing and a curse. The prophet Isaiah knew that as he spoke the recorded words in this Old Testament lesson. He urged his people to remember, hope in the midst of despair. He encouraged them not to forget the need to move in the midst of their encampment, and he sparked their homeward feelings as they sat glued to the land in exile.

The real meaning of this beautiful text from Isaiah is that *God always remembers us.* He never forgets. When he remembers, he acts on our behalf and makes us remember, too. Then he leads us to learn from what we remember. When we do not learn from what we remember, we hold grudges, and they eat us away from within. God's gift of faith is blocked, and we sit in the dust of exile forever.

Isaiah was speaking to people discouraged for so long they were comfortable in their discouragement. They had forgotten any other feeling but that deep-down sense of being lost and forgotten. Most of the time they covered those feelings with busy little tasks, just the way the Bourbon king Louis fixed clocks to forget how abandoned he felt inside.

We all feel a little lost and forgotten. Parents feel it when their children go away and don't write or call as often as they'd like. We feel it when a birthday goes by and we don't get cards the way we'd like. I remember the year I spent as a novice in the Paulist Fathers, sequestered on 1,300 desolate acres in northern New Jersey with twenty-nine other novices and a few owls at night for companionship. Christmas came. Boxes of presents rolled in from all over the country. When December 25th rolled around, I had one box: twenty-four Christmas cards! I felt lost and forgotten that day, as everyone else revelled in their gifts. They had been remembered. I hadn't. A few days later, my care package arrived, but I still went through three or four days of "they don't care; they have forgotten me."

God never forgets us. No matter how often we forget God or forget each other, he never forgets us. It has taken me a long time to believe that, but I believe it now. I hope I will never lose that belief, because I know how much it feels like a post hole digger in the stomach to feel forgotten.

Luther said some beautiful things about this passage from Isaiah when he was lecturing to those seminary students, as Margaret of Angouleme was marrying Henry of Bourbon, Duke of Navarre. Luther said, "It is the church's function through the Gospel to gather the scattered people to the sound faith." (LW 17, 179) When someone forgets me, I feel scattered. Isn't it a wonderful insight to see the purpose of church as gathering us when we feel scattered? Church exists to remember us when we feel forgotten; or it doesn't exist at all.

A large part of pastoral ministry is remembering and visiting people. This is what we all do as the church. One of my most constant concerns as a pastor is that I cannot remember people enough, so some people feel forgotten.

Why does God allow us to have these forgotten feelings? Why do we, like the Bourbons, forget nothing and learn nothing? Why do we get eaten up from inside by what we will not forget? Luther taught that this is our condition as Christians:

to feel ourselves forsaken. In real desolation, we lift our heads from the midst of the waves, for although we feel forsaken and forgotten, we know the promise of God is ours. God deserts us only to put us to the test. He shows us the power of his Word so we may trust in him. (LW 17, 184)

Isaiah believed this. Exile was God's way of testing his people. Will we trust in him? Will we sit, stuck in the mud of despair, or will we drink from the springs where he leads us?

How consoling, the power of God's memory, who acts on my behalf, who remembers. But God never remembers to stir up an old grudge. Instead, he keeps us in mind to keep us close to his heart. "Even though a mother should forget her suckling child," says the Lord, "yea, even though she should forget, I will not forget you." (49:15)

Leviticus 19:1-2, 9-18   *Epiphany 8*

Boundaries or Frontiers?

In his marvelous account, *The Rise and Fall of the Third Reich*, William L. Shirer notes how in 1942 Hitler had stretched his frontiers so wide in Russia that he simply could not defend them anymore. Ignoring Field General Franz Halder's advice, the Fuhrer dismissed him saying, "We need National Socialist ardor now, not professional ability. I cannot expect this of an officer of the old school such as you." Halder later described the Furhrer as "no longer a responsible warlord, but a political fanatic." The more Hitler's vision of the Thousand Year Reich took over, the more he sought to enslave the world in his boundaries.

    Yet, boundaries do have their place. Every day I drive along wide, round curves with well-defined lanes on my way to the church. Just the other morning, I spied a red Camaro in my rear view mirror. "Here comes trouble," I thought, "I'd better slow down to let him pass me." This man had never negotiated those curves before. Had I been parallel to him when he had trouble with the curve, our fenders, tires, and doors would have merged in a resounding crash of steel, rubber, plastic, and glass.

    Boundaries can keep us from crashing into each other, but they cannot keep us moving along. God has to give us frontiers to keep us moving. First he sets our boundaries; then he brings us to his frontiers.

    Moses was a boundary man. After he had killed an overlord

in Egypt, he ran away to hide in Midian. A man with great potential, he isolated himself as a shepherd watching his father-in-law's flocks. Although Moses didn't know it, God was drawing in this young man's fences until he hardly had breathing room for himself or his sheep.

Then God intervened. "Take off your shoes," he said, "you're standing on holy ground. I will take away the boundaries in your life and move you to a frontier. Now, get up, go, back to Egypt, and let my people go." (Exodus 3)

When God, through Moses, led his people out of Egypt, he removed their boundaries, too. After many harvests, a great chain of slavery weighed down God's people there. God sent Moses to strike down that boundary of bondage for a frontier of freedom. Through Moses, God led them through the desert to the Promised Land.

At a certain point in their wanderings in the desert, the people of Israel grew discontented. They wanted to go back. "Better to live in slavery," they cried, "than to die in this desert freedom." How we hate God's removing our boundaries for his boundless frontiers.

God told his people he wanted them separated from all that enslaved them. Even though they preferred bondage, God did not tolerate their preference. He led them to the bread of freedom, tasted first in the howling desert.

What marked the free man? "You shall not take vengeance or bear any grudge against the sons of your own people, but you shall love your neighbor as yourself: I am the Lord." Revenge enslaves us, so hold no grudges. As God works in our lives to remove our hatreds and grudges, we begin to learn to love . . . we begin to feel free.

Martin Luther struggled with boundaries all his life. God led him to the boundary of the monastery when he was twenty-one. Why? Did God want him to ache for freedom? Did he want this young peasant's son to yearn for a world that included the use and ownership of property, relationships with women, and making decisions for himself? None of these were options in the monastery.

After years of living in those enslaving monastic walls and thinking that he loved it (just as the Israelites thought they loved the slavery of Egypt more than the freedom of the desert), Luther came to see how self-destructive those boundaries were. God had to break down Luther's love for restriction to bring him to the frontier of faith.

God first compels us to despair of ourselves so we may learn to trust in his Word alone. Freed by God's promise, we are led to faith. As God shapes faith in our hearts, we experience freedom from bondage so we can be joyful, high-spirited, and eager in our relationships with God and with all people.

Freedom's frontier challenges the more restrictive limit, the lesser circumference, the tighter circle. God leads us through our deserts of bondage so we will long for faith. There he calls us to be holy as he is holy, separated from all that enslaves us.

When I went to Europe to pursue my doctoral studies, I had planned a restricted thesis — just an elaboration of my earlier study on John Calvin. About six months into my studies, a book appeared in German, a doctoral thesis by a Dutch priest from Nijmegen on the exact topic I had chosen. I was crestfallen. "Do I stop here?" I asked. "How can I begin all over again?" God showed me a way. He forced me to stretch my boundaries beyond my master's research to find Luther.

God always stretches our boundaries. Thanks be to God for his "boundary work" in our lives. He leads us each day to the frontiers of faith where alone true freedom lies.

Exodus 24:12, 15-18   **The Transfiguration of Our Lord**

Six Cloudy Days

In the early days of the University of Paris, in the eleventh and twelfth centuries, a cloud came up from Spain threatening the very fiber of Christianity. This cloud had a broad dark center of Greek pagan thought. The fleece around its edges was Arabic, for the thinkers and intellectuals who brought this cloud to Western Europe were Moslem Arabs (with names like Averroes and Avicenna). Some of them were even Jewish thinkers — somewhat surprising, since so much of Greek thought was so different from the Bible. The Greeks, for instance, spoke of God as the first cause and the first mover of all things but they never spoke of a God who walked with Adam in the cool of the evening or who called to Moses out of a burning bush.

This cloud of pagan thought rained down reason on the human spirit. Everything had to be reasonable or it had no value at all. It had to make sense from a logical point of view. God called many Christian thinkers to use this reasoning. Men like Anselm, then Bishop of Canterbury in England, applied their disciplined and creative intellects to prove that the great truths of the Christian tradition were in fact rational — that it all made sense, from a logical point of view.

The prince of these great Christian thinkers was Thomas Aquinas. Born near Monte Cassino in Italy, he arrived at the University of Paris in the 1200s, when the cloud of reason was covering everything. It began to look as if Christianity was in conflict with reason and was only for fools who had no appreciation for anything reasonable. Believers lived by blind, dumb faith. God sent Thomas into the cloud to prove that faith and reason were not contradictory.

For many years I studied Thomas Aquinas and really believed that everything could be explained in a rational, harmonious way. I don't believe that any more. Reason is not the answer to everything. Not everything makes sense from a logical point of view, because reason and logic are human inventions; faith is God's.

In my own family, my younger brother was retarded and in pain, severe pain, most of his short life. I remember coming home from school one day when I was a sophomore in high school. As I picked him up to hold him, he screamed such a cry of despair, I thought he would die in my arms. Is there a rational explanation for that? Does it make sense from a reasonable point of view? God sent me into the cloud of my brother's tragic life to draw me from reason to faith.

In this Old Testament lesson, God called Moses to faith. First, Moses went to God's mountain. Once there, he stood for six days in a cloud of cold, rain, and fog. Did Moses begin to wonder, "Why did God call me here?" Only after six days of silence did God speak. In fact, God addressed a critical and chronic need that Moses and the Hebrew people had: their need for a new direction from God's promise. They were unable to trust God, turning to a golden calf and worshiping it. God had to take their leader and isolate him for six cloudy days before they were ready for God's new Word.

God works like this often. He sends us into our cloudy days. The feeling is cold. We can't move as we once did. We feel the rain like daggers in our hearts. Then God issues his summons — to do something, to learn something, to hear what we need to hear, something we have forgotten, something that will be a surprise.

I have walked twice in clouds. Once as I hiked on the Skyline Drive in Virginia, a thunderstorm burst upon the trail.

Lightning crashed above our heads, wind ripped the trees apart, and rain beat on our faces like tiny arrows from the sky. It was a terrifying place to be with absolutely no place to go for shelter.

The second time was not so terrifying. In Scotland, on Ben Nevis, clouds from the Atlantic rolled in. We had to stop dead in our tracks and remain still for fifteen or twenty minutes, until the clouds lifted. If we moved, there was a good chance we would walk off the trail and plummet to the sea below. We communicated only by voice, so thick was the fog of the cloud.

I don't like walking in clouds, but God often makes us enter them. Sometimes we will stand there for days in the cold, straining to hear his voice. In the strength of his unflagging loyalty and care we will stand and wait for the blessed day, when, at last, he will call with his Word of grace.

www.ingramcontent.com/pod-product-compliance
Lightning Source LLC
Chambersburg PA
CBHW060852050426
42453CB00008B/948